Our Local Government

Breaking Down the Problem

Leona Fowler

COMPUTER SCIENCE For the REAL World™

Rosen Classroom™

Published in 2018 by The Rosen Publishing Group, Inc.
29 East 21st Street, New York, NY 10010

Book Design: Jennifer Ryder-Talbot
Editor: Caitie McAneney

Photo Credits: Cover Darryl Brooks/Shutterstock.com; p. 4 (main) Lane V. Erickson/Shutterstock.com; p. 4, 12 (badge icon) Rauf Aliyev/Shutterstock.com; p. 7 trekandshoot/Shutterstock.com; p. 7, 16 (gavel icon) T-Kot/Shutterstock.com; p. 8 Tony Baggett/Shutterstock.com; p. 8, 20 (recycle icon) EveeKamp/Shutterstock.com; p. 11 jiawangkun/Shutterstock.com; p. 11 (bus icon) musicman/Shutterstock.com; p. 12 John Roman Images/Shutterstock.com; p. 15 MiQ/Shutterstock.com; p. 15, 19 (tree icon) The Leon King/Shutterstock.com; p. 16 sirtravelalot/Shutterstock.com; p. 19 MaxyM/Shutterstock.com; p. 20 Rawpixel.com/Shutterstock.com.

Library of Congress-in-Publication Data

Names: Fowler, Leona.
Title: Our local government: breaking down the problem / Leona Fowler.
Description: New York : Rosen Classroom, 2018. | Series: Computer Kids: Powered by Computational Thinking | Includes glossary and index.
Identifiers: LCCN ISBN 9781508137931 (pbk.) | ISBN 9781538324233 (library bound) | ISBN 9781538353257 (6pack) | ISBN 9781538352946 (ebook)
Subjects: LCSH: Local government--United States--Juvenile literature.
Classification: LCC JS331.F69 2018 | DDC 320.80973--dc23

Manufactured in the United States of America

CPSIA Compliance Information: Batch #WS18RC: For Further Information contact Rosen Publishing, New York, New York at 1-800-237-9932

Table of Contents

The U.S. Capitol building is where the lawmaking part of the federal government meets.

Government Responsibilities

There are more than 325 million people who live in the United States. How can our government take care of so many people?

There are different levels of government in the United States. They break down the responsibilities of government between them. The federal government can print money, make national laws, and handle war and peace with another nation. It is further broken into three branches that make laws, carry out laws, and uphold laws. The state government can make state laws, grant **licenses**, and manage trade in the state.

Local Government

The needs and wants of people change from state to state, which is why it's important to have state governments as well as a federal government. This is also a reason why it's important to have a local government.

Local governments have the needs of their specific communities in mind. They provide local courts, **transportation** services, medical services, and police and fire **departments**. Local governments make sure their communities have clean parks, streets, and public spaces. Local governments break down the big problem of governing so many people into smaller tasks.

Much of a local government's work is done in a town hall or city hall, such as this one.

Public works is in charge of trash and recycling collection.

Public Works

Local governments have different departments that take care of certain tasks. One of these departments is public works.

Public works usually deals with many of the public spaces in a community. They may take care of public buildings. Public buildings include post offices, schools, and town halls or city halls. Public works also takes care of streets, bridges, and highways, so people can drive, bike, and walk safely. Workers remove snow from the street, control **sewers**, and put up helpful street signs.

Buses and Rails

The transportation department helps people get from place to place. Not everyone has a car. Some people rely on buses or rail systems to get to work, school, and shopping centers.

Buses travel aboveground and pick people up from different stops. Subways are underground parts of metro or rail systems. Rail systems can get people across a busy city quickly by transporting them underground. Some sections of these rail systems are at street level. Buses and rail systems have to run smoothly because people depend on them every day.

This bus is ready to bring people downtown!

Police officers help keep neighborhoods safe.

Police Department

Police departments help **enforce** law and order in a community. Police officers often drive around streets and highways, watching for speeding or risky drivers. They make sure that people are safe from criminals.

Police also help with car crashes and other accidents. They make sure everyone is safe and write a report about the accident. They sometimes park at **construction** areas to make sure cars driving by don't hurt construction workers. People can call the police if they are in danger or feel **threatened**.

Fire Department

The fire department helps keep people safe from fires and other emergencies. Firefighters are trained to **rescue** people from buildings that have caught on fire. They also check buildings for fire **hazards** to make sure that people will be safe.

Firefighters teach people about the importance of fire safety. They often go into schools to teach kids what to do during a fire. Firefighters are also called to the scene of car crashes and other accidents. They may even help with water rescue.

Some firefighters have to help put out large wildfires.

Court cases are often tried in courtrooms like this.

Upholding the Law

There are different levels of courts in the United States. Local courts hear cases within the community. State courts often hear cases about state law **violations**. The federal Supreme Court hears cases that question the U.S. Constitution.

Local courts take care of matters such as speeding and parking tickets. People might go to a local court over violations of local laws and rules, such as building codes. Local courts often deal with family law cases, such as divorce, and criminal cases, such as theft.

Parks and Recreation

Do you have parks in your community? This is probably thanks to the parks and **recreation** department. This department oversees the creation of new parks and the **maintenance** of old parks. It makes sure playgrounds are safe, the grass is cut, and there is little garbage in the park.

The parks and recreation department is also responsible for other recreational activities, such as community festivals. They often have activities for kids and adults in sports, arts and crafts, and community service.

Parks departments plant trees like this in their parks.

Anyone in a community can volunteer to help make it a better place.

Citizens Get Involved

The local government counts on its citizens to do certain tasks, too. Volunteers help clean parks and lead recreational activities. Citizens also take part in town hall **discussions** to let the local government know their concerns.

Some citizens make petitions, or letters signed by many people in support of or against something. They may be in support of a new recycling system or more afterschool activities. Citizens who think their causes are important can work with local leaders to make change in their communities.

Breaking It Down

Local governments have the big problem of offering many services to their citizens. How do they accomplish this? The government breaks down the jobs into smaller tasks, and each department takes care of a task.

Can you think of a time in your life when you broke a big problem down into smaller tasks? Maybe you got friends to help you do each task. What is one problem you'd like to tackle in your community? There is no problem too big when you learn how to break it down!

Glossary

construction: Having to do with the act of building something.

department: A division of a government with a specific purpose.

discussion: To talk about a certain topic.

enforce: To make sure people obey the law.

hazard: Something that may cause danger.

license: A piece of paper that shows someone is allowed to do something.

maintenance: The upkeep of land or buildings.

recreation: Having to do with fun or relaxation.

rescue: To free a person or thing from unsafe conditions.

sewer: A system for carrying away water and waste.

threatened: At risk of danger.

transportation: Having to do with taking people from one place to another.

violation: The act of ignoring someone's rights. Also, the act of breaking a law.

Index